GOLDEN GIRLS

COLORING

QUOTES

STANLEY, YOU'RE ONE CHROMOSOME AWAY

FROM BEING A POTATO.

AFTER 80, EVERY YEAR WITHOUT A HEADSTONE IS A MILESTONE!

I could get herpes listening to this story!

It's like we say in St. Olaf — Christmas without fruitcake is like St. Sigmund's Day without the headless boy.

YOU KNOW WHAT THEY SAY:
YOU CAN LEAD A HERRING TO WATER, BUT YOU HAVE TO WALK REALLY FAST OR HE'LL DIE.

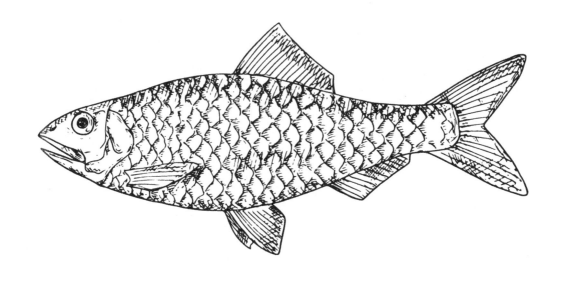

No matter how bad things get, remember these sage words:

You're old, you sag, get over it.

IT'S WONDERFUL DATING IN MIAMI. EVERY SINGLE MAN UNDER EIGHTY SELLS COCAINE.

IT'S LIKE LIFE IS A GIANT WEENIE ROAST, AND I'M THE BIGGEST WEENIE!

I HATE TO ADMIT IT,

BUT HE MELTS MY HAAGEN-DAZS.

Dorothy, was Sophia naked just now or does her dress really need ironing?

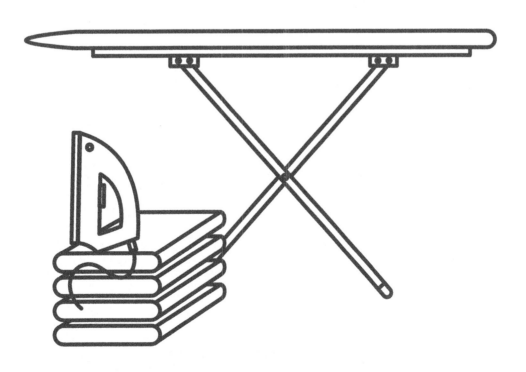

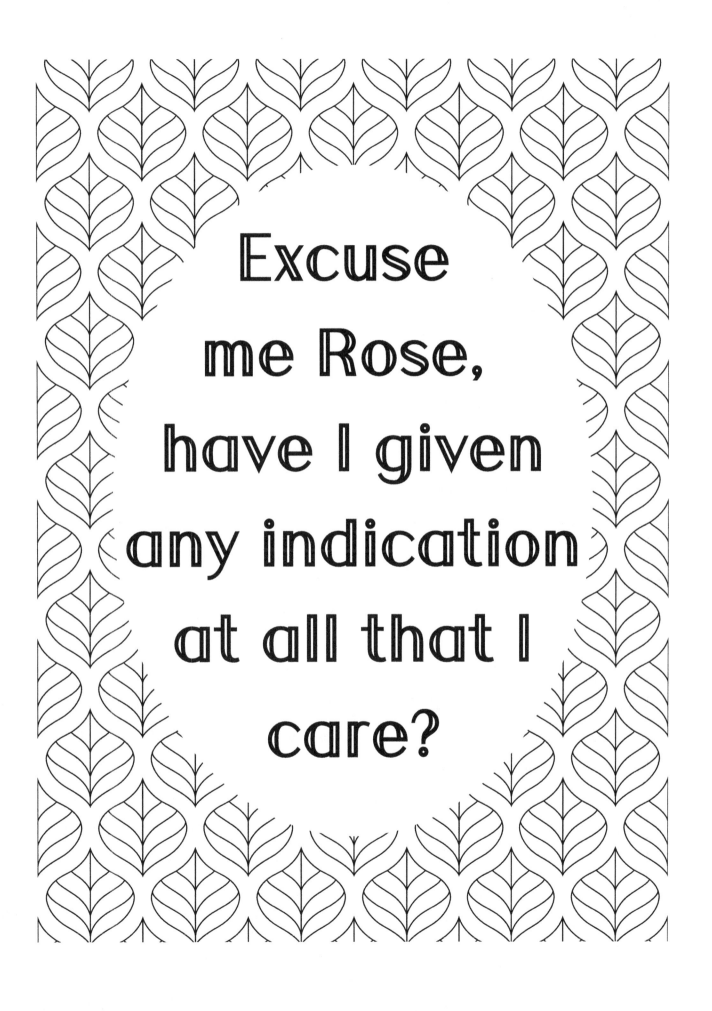

HOW COME WHENEVER MY SHIP COMES IN

IT'S LEAKING?

BETTER

LATE

THAN

I THOUGHT YOU WORE TOO MUCH MAKEUP AND WERE A SLUT. I WAS WRONG. YOU DON'T WEAR TOO MUCH MAKEUP.

WHEN A 22-YEAR-OLD GIRL MARRIES A MAN WHO'S 80, CHANCES ARE SHE IS NOT AFTER HIS BODY.

Nobody ever believes me when I'm telling the truth. I guess it's the curse of being a devastatingly beautiful woman.

IF I MET A MAN WHO WAS OVER SEVENTY BUT STILL LOOKED HALF-WAY DECENT, I'D BE ON MY BACK FASTER THAN YOU COULD SAY,

I'VE FALLEN AND I CAN'T GET

I'VE BEEN HAVING A GOOD TIME, AND THERE WASN'T EVEN A MAN IN THE ROOM.

Get back here,

you deceitful little Sicilian gecko!

It's time I gave something back to the chicken community.

A chicken once saved my life.

SHADY PINES, MA!